Britta Teckentrup

BIRDS AND THEIR FEATHERS

PRESTEL   Munich · London · New York

The Feather

A Natural Wonder

Feathers are among the most remarkable things
ever made by nature. They are delicate, complex,
extravagant, beautiful and strong – all at the same
time. All birds have feathers, which make them
unique in the animal kingdom.
Feathers enable birds to soar across the skies.
Humankind has always dreamed of flying like
a bird, and the feather has been an object of
fascination to people since the beginning of time.

Plumology

Bird Feather Science or Plumage Science

Feathers come in an amazing variety of colours and
shapes. The study of feathers is called plumology,
which is a branch of ornithology – the study of birds.
Plumage (Latin: *pluma* 'feather') refers to the layers
of feathers that cover the bird, as well as the feathers'
arrangement, pattern and colour.

Plumage feathers come in a variety of types: there are
contour feathers that cover head, neck, and body of the
bird; tail feathers; wing feathers; and the downs that
lie underneath the contour feathers.

The combined weight of all the feathers on a bird can
be three times the weight of its skeleton!

Development of the Feather

Keratin

A feather develops much like a strand of hair or a finger nail. All three are made from the protein keratin – a very strong and light material. These qualities make feathers perfect for birds, as they need to be very lightweight in order to fly. The beak and the claws of a bird are also made from keratin, and its bones are hollow. Just like our hair, feathers develop in a specialised area in the skin called a follicle. But unlike human hair, a growing feather branches into a beautiful, complex structure. Tiny muscles at the base of the feather enable the bird to move its feathers around. A bird can raise and lower its feathers, twist them or pull them closer together.

Whilst a new feather grows, it is connected to the bird's blood supply. It is disconnected once it's fully formed and can't be repaired. A fully developed feather can only be replaced by growing a new one, which is why birds spend so much time preening (cleaning) their feathers.

Structure of the Feather

Tail and Wing Feathers

Barbu

Barbicels

Barb

A feather's body looks something like a tree.
The two main parts of the feather are the shaft and the vanes.
The hollow shaft is the central support that runs all the way to the top
of the feather.
The upper part of the shaft, called the rachis, contains the feather's veins;
and the base of the shaft is known as the quill or calamus. The vanes
extend outward from each side of the shaft, giving the feather
its shape. Each vane is made up of delicate structures called
barbs. On the wing and tail feathers, the barbs
are subdivided into barbules – which sometimes
number in the hundreds on a single barb.
Most barbules have tiny hooks at the end
called barbicels that connect the
neighbouring barbs. They hook so closely
together that they form a smooth and
remarkably stiff, hard surface, which helps
maintain a feather's durable, streamlined,
windproof and aerodynamic
surface.

Quill/Calamus

Shaft

Rachis

Vanes

Wing and tail feathers are very strong, as they have to push hard against air so the birds can take off. Flight feathers are asymmetrical, with one side being thinner than the other. This enables air to flow over the wings to give a bird more lift.

Most tail feathers have the same interlocking structure as wing feathers. Arranged in a fan shape, tail feathers act as a rudder and assist with steering, balance and braking. Most birds have 12 tail feathers, which get more asymmetrical towards the outer sides. Only the two most central feathers are attached to bone. In some birds, tail feathers have evolved into showy ornaments that are useless in flight.

Types of Feathers

Down Feathers & Semiplumes

Down feathers look quite different from wing and tail feathers. They are small, soft and fluffy, and they're found under the body feathers of a bird. Downs have little or no central rachis, and their barbs twist randomly without interlocking – which makes it possible for them to trap air and insulate the bird from cold and heat. When birds fluff their feathers in the cold, it's their way of adding extra air to trap body heat and stay warmer. Semiplumes are similar to downs and are mostly hidden beneath the contour feathers, but their tips can also be visible and provide colour. Slightly larger than downs, the fluffy semiplumes have a developed central rachis with no hooks on their barbules. Semiplumes can fill in or smooth out the contour of a bird, thus helping it to fly more efficiently. Many male birds use semiplumes in courtship displays to attract a female.

Types of Feathers

Contour Feathers, Filoplumes and Bristles

Contour feathers are the visible feathers that cover and streamline a bird's body. They are arranged in an overlapping pattern. Their waterproof tips are exposed to the outside and the fluffy bases are tucked close to the body. In some birds, these strong and ridged feathers can be brightly coloured and help the bird show off. In others, they can be very plain or textured to help camouflage the animal.

Contour feathers called coverts cover the bony part of the wing and smooth over the region where the flight feathers attach to the bone – making the wing more aerodynamic.

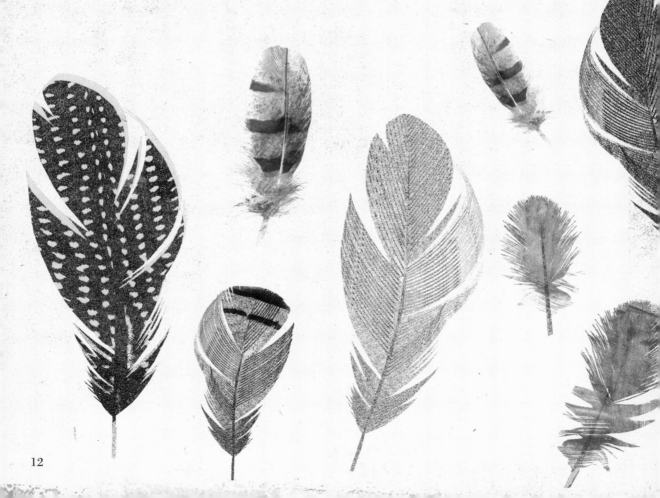

Filoplumes are short, simple feathers with few barbs. They have a fine, hair-like structure with a long shaft and only a few barbs at their tips. Scientists believe birds use their filoplumes to detect and adjust flight feathers that are out of position, thus helping the animals fly more efficiently.

Bristles are the simplest feathers. They are tiny, strong feathers with a stiff rachis and no barbs. Bristles are mainly found on the head of a bird and may protect the bird's eyes and face – a little bit like eyelashes.

The bristle feathers over a woodpecker's nostrils may function as a filter to protect the bird from dust when it pecks holes into a tree.

The Colours of Feathers

Pigment Colours – (Parrots)

Most feathers get their colours from pigments – just like our own hair. The combination of different pigments results in a specific feather colour. The pigment melanin produces black, reddish browns and pale yellows. Melanin also makes the feather denser and more resistant to rain and humidity. The darker the colour, the stronger the feather – that is why wing feathers or their tips are so often black. Carotenoid produces red, orange and yellow feathers. Birds absorb this pigment from the plants they eat. Porphyrin produces pinks, browns, reds, and greens.

The feather of a bird is often coloured differently on the inside than the outside. The visible outside of a feather is often brightly coloured or camouflaged. The inside of a feather needs colours that help protect it and keep it durable. Such colours may include red and yellow, which can prevent bacteria from harming the feather.

The Colours of Feathers

Structural Colours

Colours not caused by pigment are called structural
colours. The feathers of peacocks, hummingbirds,
kingfishers or starlings shimmer and change colour
if you look at them from different angles. This feature
is known as iridescence. Iridescent colours occur because
of the way light waves bend when they strike certain
feathers. Not all structural colours are iridescent,
however. The colour of a blue jay may appear blue
from any angle and in almost any light. When light
strikes a blue feather, the blue colour is reflected back
to the eye while all the other colours are absorbed by
a layer of melanin. But if the feather is lit from behind,
it will appear brown. The blues are lost because light is
no longer reflected off the front of the feather. Instead,
the brownish colours of the melanin protein
become visible to the eye.

Pink Feathers

Flamingo

The flamingo obtains its wonderful pink colour from the food it eats – crustaceans. Without this diet, which is rich in pink carotenoid pigments, the flamingo's feathers would be white or gray.

The Longest and the Shortest Feather

The longest and widest tail feathers of a wild bird belong to the crested argus pheasant (*Rheinhardia ocellata*), which can reach the length of 173 centimetres (68 inches) and width of 13 centimetres (5 inches).

There is also an ornamental breed of chicken, the Onagadori, which is bred to grow extremely long tail feathers of more than 10 metres (34 feet) in length! It can't fly, but it looks very pretty.

The smallest feathers belong to the smallest bird, the bee hummingbird (*Mellisuga helenae*) of Cuba. This animal measures just 5.7 centimetres (2 ¼ inches) long, including bill and tail. You would need a magnifying device see its individual feathers!

How Many Feathers?

The ruby-throated hummingbird (*Archilochus colubris*) has a beautiful and colourful plumage made from around 940 feathers.

The tundra swan (*Cygnus columbianus*) can have up 25,000 feathers in the cold winter. Birds that live in cold areas can possess 50 percent more feathers in the winter than they can in the summer.

Penguins have more feathers than most birds: about 100 per square inch. Penguin feathers are so dense and overlapping that they almost look like hair or skin.

Evolution of the Feather

Many scientists believe birds evolved from dinosaurs. Various fossil discoveries of feathered dinosaurs in recent years seem to support the theory that birds descended from two-legged, ground-running dinosaurs called thero-pods – the dinosaur group that included *Tyrannosaurus rex* and *Velociraptor*.

The search for the ancestors of modern birds began when fossils of *Archaeopteryx*, the first known bird, was discovered in 1861. *Archaeopteryx* had feathers and other traits of living birds along with signs of a reptilian past, such as teeth in its mouth, claws on its wings, and a long, bony tail. Despite all these discoveries, however, scientists still don't know exactly how dinosaurs first took to flight.

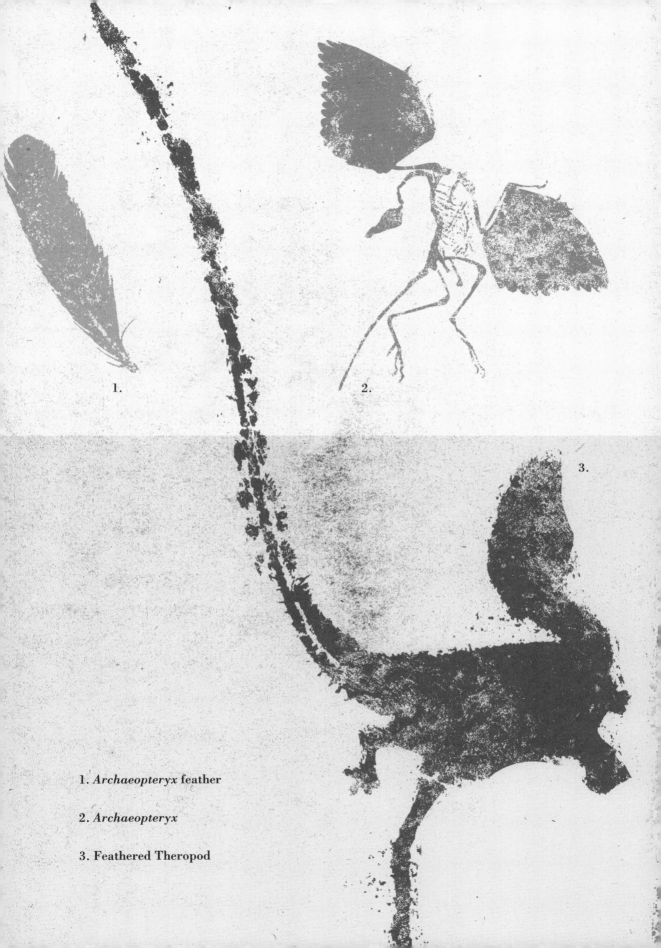

1. *Archaeopteryx* feather

2. *Archaeopteryx*

3. Feathered Theropod

Flying

Almost 40 different functions and uses of the feather are known to ornithologists (bird scientists).

One of the primary functions is flight. Without feathers birds would not be able to fly. Feathers help birds move air with every flap, so they can lift themselves off the ground. As the bird moves forward, air moves faster over the wing and slower under the wing. This difference in pressure creates lift and lets the bird stay in the air.

When birds flap their wings, feathers help push birds forward – a phenomenon called thrust. A flight feather is asymmetrical, with one vane that is thin and stiff and another that is long and flexible. When a bird tilts its wings, its flight feathers enable it to adjust air flow below and above the wings, thus generating lift.

A bird has primary and secondary wing feathers. The secondaries, or remiges, are attached to the bone with strong ligaments so they can withstand the demands of flight and be precisely positioned. The primaries are the longest wing feathers and are attached to the outer part of the wing. Their position can be controlled by the bird.

Wing types

The Fast Take Off & the Elliptical Wing

Birds have different ways of taking off and flying, which require wings of different shapes and size.

Some birds, including pheasants and grouse, need to take off quickly to escape predators. They have relatively short and fat wings that give them the thrust to lift off in an instant. This elliptical wing shape also allows for twisting flight at short distances to avoid trees and other obstacles. Birds with short, rounded wings are very good at manoeuvring in tight spaces, such as dense vegetation. But this wing shape isn't good for long or high-speed flight.

Wing types

The Broad & Thin Soaring Wing

Soaring birds over land tend to have broad, long wings. This wing type is characteristic of black and turkey vultures, red-tailed hawks, broad-winged hawks, storks, northern harriers, condors, etc. Turkey vultures (*Cathartes aura*) can soar for hours without flapping their wings by catching warm,

rising air. This uplifting of warm air is known as a thermal. Soaring wings often have spread-out single feathers that look like fingers at the end of the wing, which help to catch the thermals and allow for subtle movements without flapping the whole wing. Soaring flight takes very little energy, as the birds don't have to flap their wings very often. Soaring birds like gulls, gannets and albatrosses have to apply a different technique over water, where air thermals don't form. They need to make the best possible use of wind. Their wings, therefore, are both long and very thin – perfect for a bird's life at sea.

Wing types

The High-Speed Wing

With its long, slender, angled shape, the high-speed wing
type is great for fast movements because it has very little
air resistance. It is characteristic of swifts, swallows,
ducks and many shorebirds.
The triangular and swept-back shape of these wings looks
a little bit like the wings of a high-speed jet fighter.

Wing types

The Slow, Flapping Wing

The flight of herons, egrets, and ibises is characterized by long, slow wing flaps. Their wings are long, arched and relatively slender. This wing shape is good for long flights but is not good for quick manoeuvring or quick take-offs.

Hovering

Several bird species use hovering. Hummingbirds
are such accomplished hoverers, it looks as if they're
floating in space when they drink nectar from flowers.
The hummingbird's flight is unique. Its wing is
extended throughout the whole stroke and creates a
symmetrical figure of eight, with the wing producing
lift on both the up- and down-strokes. Some hummingbirds can beat their wings 52 times a second!
The ability to hover is usually confined to smaller birds,
but some larger birds such as kites or ospreys can also
hover for a short period of time.

Gliding

Gliding is done without any effort at all – no propulsion or thrust is used. When air moves over the top of the curved bird's wing, it has a longer distance to travel than the air moving underneath the wing. This means that it produces less pressure above the wing than the air

does underneath the wing, which keeps the bird aloft. By tilting its wings a bird can change speed while gliding. An albatross can glide hundreds of miles without flapping. A wandering albatross is one of the most amazing flyers on our planet. It has the longest wingspan of any bird – almost 3.5 metres (12 feet). These large sea birds can travel 15,000 kilometres (around 10,000 miles) over the sea before returning to land.

Flapping

Many birds use both flapping and gliding to fly.
A northern cardinal (*Cardinalis cardinalis*) will flap
several times, then glide for a short distance and
repeat this pattern as it flies. Flapping is a quite
complicated process. Birds have to create their own
thrust to move themselves through the air, but they
must also keep the air resistance created by their
wings and body to a minimum. That is why a bird
changes the angle of its wings and partially folds
them up on the upstroke when they flap.

Quiet Feathers

The Silent Flight of the Owl

If you see an owl fly through the night sky, it won't seem to make a sound. The quietness of their flight enables an owl to fly close to their prey without being detected. Owls have specialised primary feathers on the edge of their wings, their leading edge being serrated rather than smooth, a little bit like a comb. This means that the sound of turbulence that usually occurs when air rushes over a bird's wing is reduced by these specially adapted feathers. Other features of an owl's body also support its silent flight. Its dense, velvety plumage helps absorb sound, and its large wings and relatively small body enable it to glide through the skies with very small wing beats.

Feathers for Water Birds

Feathers have many different functions apart from enabling the bird to fly. Using the trapped air in their downy feathers, water birds like ducks or swans can float on water. The downy feathers also provide protection from cold water. Other types of feathers can also keep water out. Contour feathers are arranged in an overlapping pattern showing only the waterproof, oil-coated tip, which enables the water to run off the bird. Unlike many other birds that are born 'naked', the chicks of water birds hatch with a full coat of downy feathers, as they have to swim almost immediately. However, the feathers of a new-born chick aren't waterproof, and its mother has to apply a protective coat of oil on the chick before its first swim.

Feathers for Display

Feather colours, patterns and shapes send visual signals to potential mates
or rivals. In the breeding season, a male bird performs spectacular and
colourful displays to attract a female. Most female birds are attracted
to the male with the showiest feathers and the most energetic display.
Feathers have evolved into many different shapes and colours for
display purposes. In some birds, like the peacock, tail feathers have
grown into impressive ornaments that are useless in flight.
Some feathers have evolved so much that they don't even look
like feathers any more. These include the ornamental tail feathers
of the male king bird-of-paradise (*Cicinnurus regius*). Birds-of-paradise
have some of the most spectacular courtship displays of all birds.

Not all showy feathers are used to attract a partner; some are used
in displays of aggression and defence.

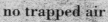

no trapped air

trapped air

Protection from Cold, Heat and Sunrays

The amount of air trapped between the soft downs of a bird insulates it from cold and heat. The bird can regulate its body temperature by adding or removing air. Air traps the bird's body heat – the more trapped air, the warmer the bird.

Feathers also protect the bird from the sun, and darker-coloured feathers can offer further protection.

Feathers are used to provide shade. An adult ostrich employs its feathers and wings to shield its young from the hot sun.

Snowshoeing

Some birds are completely covered with feathers and even have feather-covered feet in the winter. These include the rock ptarmigan (*Lagopus muta*) and willow ptarmigan (*Lagopus lagopus*), grouse that live in the Arctic snow. Feet feathers make it easier for the birds to walk on the snow without sinking down. They increase the size of their feet and work just like snowshoes. The feathers also help to keep the birds' feet warm in extremely cold weather.

Feathers as Climbing Aids

Some birds use their tail feathers as supports
when on the ground or climbing trees.
The stiff tail feathers of a woodpecker enable
it to brace itself on a tree as it climbs.

Singing Feathers

Some birds can make different sounds generated by their feathers. The male club-winged manakin (*Machaeropterus deliciosus*) of Central and South America can 'sing' a tune with his specially adapted feathers in each wing. When a manakin shakes its wings, these feathers create sounds by rubbing against one another.

Feathers as Hearing Aids

Some birds, especially owls, have their face feathers arranged to form two large discs around their eyes. Those facial discs help them locate prey more accurately in the dark as sounds are channelled into their ears.

Pollination

A hummingbird can help pollinate flowers. When a hummingbird drinks nectar from a flower, the feathers around its head pick up pollen. When it flies to the next flower, the pollen is transferred. This process helps the plants to reproduce.

Feathers for Keeping Clean

Some birds, like herons, have small feathers called powder down. They can crush the powder down with their beak or feet and rub it into their plumage. This helps keep the feathers conditioned, and it may also help to control parasites.

Digestion and Nest Building

Some fish-eating birds eat their own feathers to line their stomachs, which protects them from sharp fish bones and makes it easier to regurgitate the bones.

Feathers are also used as soft nesting material. Many birds line their nests with feathers – especially sea birds. The feathers help insulate the nest and keep the eggs warm.

Carrying Water

The Special Feathers of the Sandgrouse

The sandgrouse lives in the hot desert and has developed
special belly feathers that can soak up and hold water.
With these feathers, the sandgrouse can transport water
to its nest to nourish its chicks or cool down its eggs.

Escaping Predators

Losing a tail feather sometimes helps a bird escape from a predator. The bird is able to drop some of its tail feathers when it's under attack or frightened – an action called fright moult.

Feathers for Camouflage

Many birds have feathers that help them blend into their surroundings so that predators cannot see them. When the bird is a predator, camouflaged feathers help it stay hidden from its prey. In forest environments, patterned brown contour feathers can provide impressive camouflage, imitating bark, branches or leaves. The feathers of the snowy owl (*Bubo scandiacus*) are snow-white in winter and help the bird to blend perfectly into the arctic snow. In the summer, its white plumage is covered with brown dots to mimic the look of the arctic landscape after snow has melted.

Camouflage can also be bright. The bright green eclectus parrot (*Eclectus roratus*) is perfectly camouflaged against the lush green rain forest canopy.

Preening & Moulting

A bird must look after its feathers, as they are vital for its survival. It uses its beak to make sure the interlocking structure of the feathers isn't disturbed. Feathers that aren't hooked together properly will cause problems. Most birds have special oil in a preen gland (also called the uropygial gland) located near the tail. They use their beaks to apply this oily substance to the feathers, which makes them waterproof and keeps them moist and flexible. The process of grooming is called preening. But even though birds look after their plumage very carefully, a feather is a dead structure and cannot repair itself when damaged. Because a healthy and functional coat is critical to survival, most birds shed their old feathers and grow a whole new set at least once a year. This process is called moulting.

For most songbirds, moulting takes five to twelve weeks. They shed only a few feathers at a time and are still able to fly. The number of times moulting occurs each year varies amongst birds.

The Feather in Culture
& Mythology

In many cultures, feathers were regarded as both ceremonial and decorative and symbolised humankind's wish to fly and reach higher levels. For ancient Egyptians, a person's soul had to be as light as a feather to pass the judgement of Ma'at – the Egyptian goddess of truth, justice and the underworld. She is often portrayed as wearing an ostrich feather, the symbol of truth, on her head.

Feathered and winged creatures appear in many cultures and their mythologies. They include Pegasus, the white winged horse of ancient Greece; the griffin, a half-eagle and half-lion creature; the Greek sphinx, with its human head, lion body, and bird's wings; the Assyrian lamassu, a winged bull; or the thunderbird in Native American mythology.

Fairy tales like the brothers Grimm's 'The Three Feathers', 'The Golden Bird' or 'The Golden Goose' also have feathers as a central image.

Native Americans

The image of the feather and the feather headdress is instantly associated with Native American culture.

A feather can represent honour, strength, trust, wisdom, power, freedom and much more. Feathers were given as a sign of respect and honour and were a symbol of strength.

Native Americans believe that every bird species has its own character traits that can be passed on to humans through the feathers. All natural things in the universe, including birds, feathers, plants or rocks, have spirits and possess power and wisdom. The many different Native American tribes all developed their own unique beliefs and rituals.

Eagle feathers have great cultural and spiritual value to Native Americans in the USA and First Nations peoples in Canada.

Human Usage of the Feather

People have used bird feathers for thousands of years. During the Stone Age, they were important for making arrows. Today, manufacturers use insulating down feathers to fill pillows, blankets, mattresses, sleeping bags or quilted coats. Feathers of domestic birds are used in fashion and for other ornamental purposes. There was a booming international trade in plumes during the 18th, 19th, and even 20th centuries due to the fashion of extravagant feathered hats for women. Certain feathers could fetch extremely high prices. The hunting of wild birds for these ornamental feathers endangered some species, like the great egret (*Ardea alba*). Conservationists led a major campaign against the use of feathers in hats, and eventually the fashion changed.

The Quill

Quills were used for writing with ink from the 6th to the 19th century, before the invention of the metal pen.
They helped people write medieval manuscripts like the Magna Carta or the Declaration of Independence.
The primary feathers of large birds, especially geese, were used to make quill pens.
The word pen comes from the Latin word 'penna', meaning feather; and the French word 'plume' can mean either feather or pen.

The Dream of Flying

Daedalus and Icarus

The story of Daedalus and Icarus is one of the best known ancient Greek myths. Daedalus and his son Icarus tried to escape from the Cretan king Minos by attaching wings to their backs. The wings were made from feathers and wax. Daedalus warned his son not to fly too close to the sun, as it would melt the wax on his wings. But Icarus grew reckless and ignored his father's advice. The sun melted the wax and his wings fell apart, plunging Icarus into the sea, where he drowned.

The Dream of Flying

Flying Machines

The famous Renaissance man Leonardo da Vinci (1452–1519) was a painter, architect and inventor, and he was fascinated by all things scientific. At the beginning of the 16th century, he wrote the 'Codex on the Flight of Birds'. His drawing of a primitive helicopter and airplane demonstrated his advanced understanding of aerodynamics and flight more than 500 years ago.

The first flying machines merely imitated the appearance of birds without understanding their biological and physical structure. Daredevil inventors simply attached wings to their arms and jumped off roofs, bridges or cliffs – many dying in the process.

In 1853, English inventor George Cayley built the world's first glider. It flew 183 metres (600 feet) before it crash-landed.

In 1891, inspired by Cayley, German inventor Otto Lilienthal built smaller gliders that were steered by the weight of the pilot. With them, he managed to make 2,000 controlled 'flights', gliding more than 200 metres (820 feet) by launching himself off a hill.

He was a big inspiration to Orville and Wilbur Wright, the American pioneers who built a static wing construction with a petrol motor. In 1903, the Wright brothers made the first truly successful airplane flight. In 1909, French aviator Louis Blériot completed the first powered flight across the English Channel.

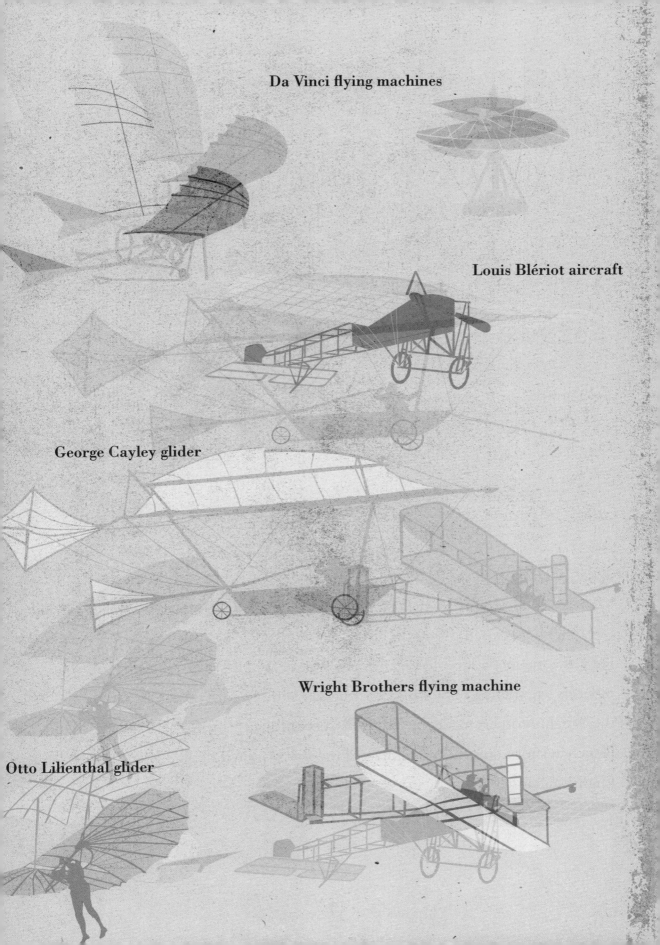

Da Vinci flying machines

Louis Blériot aircraft

George Cayley glider

Wright Brothers flying machine

Otto Lilienthal glider

The Feather on the Moon

There is still a feather on the moon – a falcon feather –
dropped by astronaut David Scott during the Apollo 15
mission in 1971 and left there ever since.

Scott dropped both the feather and a hammer to demons-
trate a famous idea by the 17th-century Italian scientist
Galileo Galilei. Galileo had argued that objects of different
sizes and weights would fall at the same speed in a vacuum
(where there was no air resistance). This idea eventually led
to the Law of Gravity, developed by English scientist Isaac
Newton.

When Scott dropped the feather and the hammer at the
same time, the lack of gravity and air resistance on the
moon enabled both objects to reach the moon's surface
at the same time. Galileo was proven right again!

© 2018, Prestel Verlag, Munich · London · New York
A member of Verlagsgruppe Random House GmbH
Neumarkter Strasse 28   81673 Munich

Prestel Publishing Ltd.
14-17 Wells Street
London W1T 3PD

Prestel Publishing
900 Broadway, Suite 603
New York, NY 10003

In respect to links in the book, the Publisher expressly notes
that no illegal content was discernible on the linked sites at the
time the links were created. The Publisher has no influence at all
over the current and future design, content or authorship of the
linked sites. For this reason the Publisher expressly disassociates
itself from all content on linked sites that has been altered since
the link was created and assumes no liability for such content.

Library of Congress Control Number: 2017950212
A CIP catalogue record for this book is available
from the British Library.

Editorial direction: Doris Kutschbach
Copyediting: Brad Finger
Production management: Astrid Wedemeyer
Typesetting: textum GmbH, Feldafing
Separations: ReproLine Mediateam, Munich
Printing and binding: DZS Grafik, d.o.o., Ljubljana
Paper: Tauro

Verlagsgruppe Random House FSC® N001967

Printed in Slovenia

ISBN 978-3-7913-7335-5
www.prestel.com